The Breaking & the Blooming

A collection of modern poetry from me,
to you.

The Breaking & the Blooming

Copyright © 2022 Keira Van der Kolk
All rights reserved
Illustrations by Hannah Woolley

The Breaking & the Blooming

To my mother, Stephanie,
thank you for giving me the strength.
I am proud to carry the title of your daughter.

The Breaking & the Blooming

Authors Note

Inside your palms, you hold my heart. Every emotion, thought and feeling, compacted into tiny little pages. This book contains hurt, healing, and everything in between—the most vulnerable parts of me that might be troubling to digest. I uncover my experiences with heartbreak, mental health, and trauma, but also sprinkle in my journey on self-love and acceptance. This is a project that involves many people in my life—those I know personally and those I do not. You have all encouraged me to put my words on paper so that they could sleep on your shelves or nightstands, or wherever you please. I couldn't have done this without you.

This book might contain content that could be uncomfortable or upsetting to some; please keep this in mind as you turn each page.

Yours truly, Keira.

The Breaking & the Blooming

Table of Contents

The Hurting …… pg. 6

The Heartbreak …… pg. 43

The Healing …… pg. 88

The Hurting

The Breaking & the Blooming

You see destruction
but I see survival

The Breaking & the Blooming

I bit my tongue
and swallowed my truth
because I'd rather hold it in
until my stomach aches
than say it out loud
and have you look at me
any different

The Breaking & the Blooming

I am a stranger in my own body
no longer the main inhabitant
I have shrunk myself down
to nothing
but a visitor
an intruder perhaps
and nothing has felt more lonely
than that

The Breaking & the Blooming

You called me crazy
but not the pretty kind
I must have blurred the line
between desirable
and just a little too much

The Breaking & the Blooming

All I wanted was someone who knows
that I have been hurt before
and would rather die
than ever hurt me like that
again

The Breaking & the Blooming

I watch myself set fire from a distance
to everything I have ever loved
then fall apart with the ash in my palms
like I did not hold the match
with the same two hands

The Breaking & the Blooming

It's not that
I don't want to be who I am
It just scares me to know
that I will forever be her

The Breaking & the Blooming

I think I run away from happiness
and deny it
because when it is in my grasp
it never feels like mine to keep
Like it doesn't belong to me
anyway

The Breaking & the Blooming

I am still mourning all the parts of me
that I neglected
while trying to make you love me

The Breaking & the Blooming

Sometimes I wonder
if you would have loved me
a little bit more
and a little bit louder
if I were anybody
but me

The Breaking & the Blooming

He said he loved me
I'm not so sure that's true
although my father did always used to say
the one way to tell if he likes you
is if he's mean to you
And I guess that's where it started
the mocking of the shape of my nose
the freckles on my cheeks
the size of my breasts
I mean I did bloom a little earlier than most
that must be why everyone always asked
how many boys in my class
were chasing after me
You know
typical stuff a 9-year-old would hear
being labelled the heartbreaker
before I could even spell it
So now I can't help but confuse the two
love and hate somehow both feel the same
when you're aching

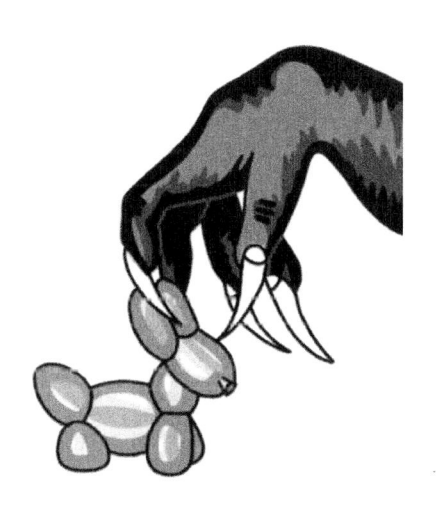

The Breaking & the Blooming

All the time
I am desired
but never *loved*

The Breaking & the Blooming

My body does not exist
just for your hands to grab
whenever they are lonely
And it's wrong of you to appear
after months of being absent
just to tell me that you miss the way my lips felt
pressed up against yours
because I am not the substitute for your vulnerability
And I want you to know
that I no longer cave into the arms of those
who once broke me

The Breaking & the Blooming

I'm afraid
that I'm not meant
to be loved
Not that I'm undeserving
or incapable
just that my purpose is to hug the devil
out of those around me
and get nothing in return
But what happens
when I fall apart
who squeezes the devil out of me
when I'm not strong enough
when my arms shrink
and I can't reach
Maybe I am ok with it
but the ones who give out all their love
usually are the ones
who need it the most

The Breaking & the Blooming

To be loved
is different
than to feel loved

The Breaking & the Blooming

You made destruction
comfortable for me
Like if the world was falling apart
it wouldn't matter to me
I wouldn't notice the rumbling beneath my feet
and if the trees were on fire
I would just remember your warmth
I hate that it's easier to settle in the wreckage
but it's all I know

The Breaking & the Blooming

My body is a graveyard
for the girl I used to be
She is no longer here
but never really gone
either
She deserves bouquets of lilies and daisies
but I don't really visit that much
anymore
And it's not that I am afraid
I am just not ready to accept
that she might not come back to me
the same way I left her

The Breaking & the Blooming

How ironic
that the time I feel most safe
is with a hand
wrapped around my neck

The Breaking & the Blooming

When I talk about death
understand I don't mean of me
there is someone else occupying this body
and I don't know how to rid their existence
without them taking me too
I do not want to die
in fact
I can find beauty in almost everything I meet
I could gaze at a dull sky for hours
and wait around until the moon takes its place
because I know just how bright she can be
Or find a field full of weeds
and dance in it like they were hydrangeas
because nobody ever believes that dandelions aren't flowers
So when I say I want to die
investigate the hesitation
take a moment to know it's not me speaking
and promise me you will search for me
she is lost in this flesh somewhere

The Breaking & the Blooming

You say you can't handle my depression
but tell me
how do you think I feel?
When you can leave whenever you please
but I am with me no matter where I go
no escape from this flesh
it is my home
You can decide which days to love me on
I must love me even if I'm collapsing
or I will crumble

And I did crumble at your feet
once before
a state of vulnerability you labeled insufferable
but how do you think I feel?
I am the one who suffers in this skin
you are just the bystander on the outside
looking in
yet you only managed to barely scratch the surface
of my severity

I've seen it all
sat front row in every devastating fall
but I've also flourished
and if you can't bear the intensity of my decline
you won't stand a chance amongst my uprise

The Breaking & the Blooming

Don't tell me you love me
until you've lived past the tear-drenched sheets on my
basement couch
I'm not talking mascara-stained cheeks
I am not the quiet pond in your front yard
I transform into the ocean at midnight
and I pour for miles
among miles
among miles
Your delicate sailboat won't reach the end
don't try that here
and your red life coat won't keep you afloat
amidst these atrocities
I'd say I resemble a natural disaster
I'm hell
but you can't keep your eyes off me
Don't tell me you love me
until you've managed to maintain your sanity
when I couldn't manage mine
And know that I'm not trying to make my tragedies
sound poetic
but do not say you love me
until you have seen the parts of me
that have been deemed unlovable

The Breaking & the Blooming

Whenever my mother asks
what is wrong
I often choke on my words
shards of glass when I try to spit them out
The fear of disappointment like weights on my throat
how do you tell the one person who gave you life
that you are suffocating in its existence?
But I assure you that I am not broken
crooked perhaps
but *never* broken
The desire to mend the sad parts of me grows inside like a
seed
each day
each breath
a water droplet
a commitment to myself
And if I am not okay today
who am I to say I won't ever be?

that possibility alone
must be enough for me

The Breaking & the Blooming

You made breathing easy
but also made me suffocate
How that is
I'll never understand

The Breaking & the Blooming

My body is supposed to be
a home
but somehow
I turned it
into a warzone

I am a different kind of lonely
the one where even in a crowded room
my soul still feels misplaced

The Breaking & the Blooming

I feel you on my skin
even after all this time
I have been showering three times a day
sometimes four
to try to erase your fingerprints
But all my skin does is burn from riddance

I hope when you look at your palms
you know they are tainted with my blood
And one day I know my body will heal from you
but yours will forever reek of sin

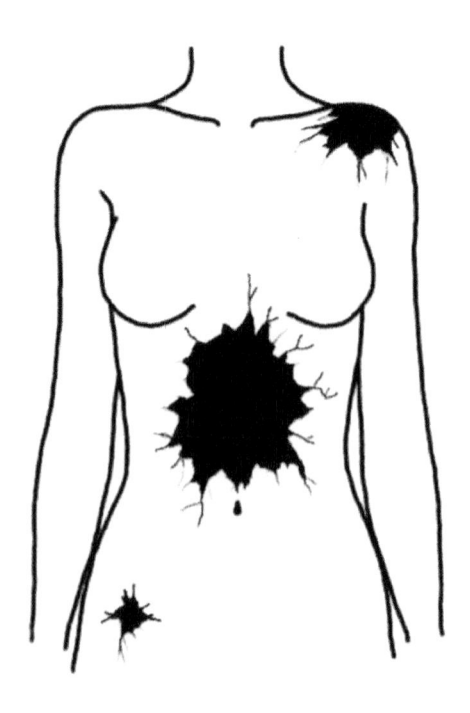

The Breaking & the Blooming

I willingly hold the broken
inside my palms
with expectations that my fingers
won't be left slit
from the shards

The Breaking & the Blooming

I cared about your happiness
more than I ever cared about my own
So much so that I forgot mine even mattered
in the first place

The Breaking & the Blooming

If the love
you have with yourself
is the most valuable love
of them all
I think I messed up
pretty bad

but I can't seem to remember when
Suddenly
I went from prancing around the yard
to wishing
I was literally nothing
at all

The Breaking & the Blooming

When I was a kid
everyone always used to ask me the same old question
what do you want to be when you grow up?
And if you asked me then
I'd say a princess
a vet
a teacher
I would spend hours in my room talking to the wall
But if you'd ask me now
I'd just say *happy*
I want to wake up in the morning
not with the sole purpose of breathing
but something to live for
I'm scared of wasting any more time
I want to meet people and be ok when they don't like me
and form relationships and not fall apart when they do
I want to see skies from different cities' points of view
and sit in family-owned coffee shops
that don't have the best coffee
but you feel at home anyway
I don't want to fear tomorrow
or regretful of yesterday
just happy

The Breaking & the Blooming

I am alive
but not in the way
I should be

The Breaking & the Blooming

After it all
they called me strong
and I felt like a fraud
My skin has never been thinner
my bones fragile as ever
one touch and I am shattered to pieces
Why do we have to be untouchable?
or tough
I still fall apart when the door shuts
I don't know how to be strong

but I do know
how to survive

The Breaking & the Blooming

Some day
me and self-love
will coexist
Some day

But for now
I observe her in the back corner
still struggling to cough up the courage
to invite her over

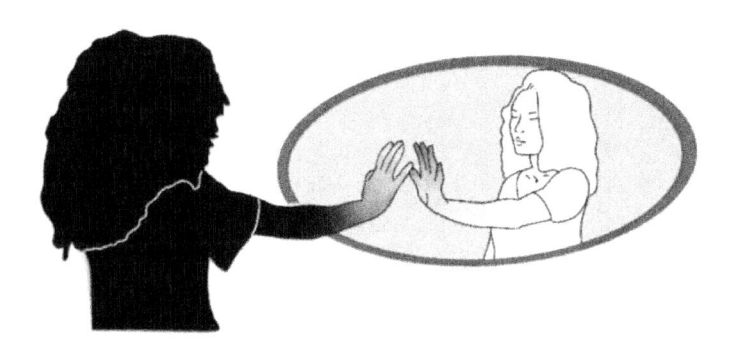

The Breaking & the Blooming

I am not afraid of love
I am simply afraid
of loss

The Breaking & the Blooming

I hate how I fight with my mother
like I am not half of her
like I didn't take far more
than just her blue eyes
I see the world exactly like she does
with anger
then hope
with anger
then hope again
She taught me resilience
but also taught me how to fall apart
and I can't tell if I resent her for it
or love her for it
But then again
to resent her
is to resent myself

The Breaking & the Blooming

I know I am not my illness
but some days
I swear that I am
I wear these traits like a robe
that I can never seem to remove
it's clinging onto my bones
And if a diagnosis is not a label
why is it embedded in my skin like ink?
Most times I forget that it's there
but one look in the mirror
and I am drowning in catastrophe

I guess I am not my illness
but what if it's all there is to me

The Heartache

The Breaking & the Blooming

It's tragic how we can lose people
when we love too much
but also
when we don't love enough
And I wonder which is worse
the feeling of knowing you would have done anything
and they still didn't stick
or that you were so close
but let it slip

The Breaking & the Blooming

He loved me enough
to undress me
but never enough to hold me
to caress me
to treat me kindly
to protect me

And that's where the idea of love
got lost for me

The Breaking & the Blooming

I don't think you and I
were ever meant to make it out
alive
or even make it out in one piece
So now here I am
mourning all the things we could have been
if we had tried a little harder
at least

The Breaking & the Blooming

Is all love tragic
or do I just make it that way

Oh God
I think I keep making it
that way

The Breaking & the Blooming

Your absence is quite unfamiliar to me
It's been months
and most mornings
I still reach over to hold you
just to get a handful
of the empty sheets

The Breaking & the Blooming

Our love consisted of me
giving you all that I had
Yet I'm here
all alone again
with nothing left
and somehow
you're still empty too

The Breaking & the Blooming

I just wanted to be something to you
without having to ask

The Breaking & the Blooming

I have reached the point in missing you
where I would give anything
to fight with you again
Even though it ripped me apart
when we did
Somehow the silence
manages to hurt more

The Breaking & the Blooming

I don't want to hate sunsets
scattered in pinks and blues
but I do
I wish you had waited to tell me
that you loved me
somewhere other than between the paths
of the sun and moon
Because how can I ever look up at the sky again
without seeing you concealed within the hues

The Breaking & the Blooming

The version of me that you know
doesn't even exist
anymore
and I can't decipher whether that's a good thing
or not
How I have grown so much
you would have to get to know me
all over again
or that now it's almost as if we never met
in the first place

The Breaking & the Blooming

Seeing the good
in everybody you meet
is both a blessing
and a curse
They could repeatedly tear you
to pieces
and all you can remember
is that you were once broken too

The Breaking & the Blooming

The difference between you and me
is I loved you despite the darkest parts of your soul
but the moment I revealed my hurt
your love was off the table

The Breaking & the Blooming

I'd rather you reach behind the bones
in my chest
with your bare hands
instead of trying to break me
from afar
I thought that after all this time
that's at least what you owe me
but sometimes we don't get
what we deserve
And I guess that's just what people like you
were made for
showing no mercy when it comes to the breaking
but can never stomach
looking you in the eyes
while doing it

The Breaking & the Blooming

I hope all of those before me
have healed
and I hope all the those after me
are capable of healing

The Breaking & the Blooming

Not all first loves
are even love at all
They either leave you wondering
how something could have been so beautiful
or will teach you
what love should never be

The Breaking & the Blooming

I was always told that you can't take back
the words you have said
So I guess the first time
you told me you loved me
is echoing somewhere in the universe still
and I can't seem to let go of that

The Breaking & the Blooming

I'm angry
that we met
when we did
When I was too broken and unhealed
to realize that not everybody is here to ruin me
Maybe you were my right person
wrong time
but does that also mean
we will meet again
That somewhere down the road our paths cross
And if they do
I'll hold you in my arms just a little tighter
and hope this time
you don't slip between the cracks

The Breaking & the Blooming

We are skin on skin
but somehow
we still feel miles apart
like there are planets between us
but I can feel your heart
We sit here
and don't speak
because there is nothing left to say
the silence speaks for itself anyway
You don't love me the way you used to
I don't love you the way I used to
yet we don't let go
because what we had

is all we have

The Breaking & the Blooming

Who made you fear love so badly
that you don't even love yourself anymore
you avoid every mirror you walk past now
Which hands made your body feel like it was only worthy of
sensual touch
no hand holding
no hair stroking
nothing unless the lights were shut off
Who convinced you that love was painful
that it's always a war between a broken soul
and one that just wants to be wanted

Love should not hurt
and if you are hurting
that is hate

The Breaking & the Blooming

The very thing that distinguishes us both
is that I wouldn't hesitate to choose you in every lifetime
but you wouldn't even choose me in this one
and although I gave you my flesh and bones
I know I cannot love you into loving me
So there you are
overflowing with my love
and here I am
pleading for a droplet of yours
or whatever I could salvage
But there must come a time when you recognize that to grieve someone
hurts a lot less than forcing them to be a part of you
And I know I should not beg for love
but just once
I wanted someone to be afraid of losing me

The Breaking & the Blooming

I wondered how I questioned your lack of love so deeply
but not once questioned my own self-hate
Perhaps it's my turn to love me
in every way I wanted you
to love me
unconditionally and without hesitation

The Breaking & the Blooming

Can we go back to who we were
that night
before the chaos
before the destruction
It's almost like all love does
is break people apart
I know it tore us
to pieces

The Breaking & the Blooming

You cannot heal someone who is too comfortable
with being broken
I learned that after I saturated your entire existence
with whatever amount of intimacy I seemed to have left
and your response was
but I never asked you to
It is certain that you drained me to my core
something I am afraid I will never have the space to regain
because although you left me empty
for some reason being whole again simply appears to be
beyond my reach
The nothingness within me is being drowned by more
nothingness
but despite this misery that resides within my bones
I still have the need to save you

That's when I knew I loved too deep
when even my love wasn't valued
I thought the only answer was to love
even harder

The Breaking & the Blooming

I am homesick for hands
that don't even know how to hold me
You praised those hands like they made flowers grow
on my skin
but all they did was touch
No array of lilacs across this body
just scattered fingerprints
that my mind begs to forget
but my heart refuses to let go of

The Breaking & the Blooming

When I think about our love
the only metaphor that seems to escape from my mind
is that you are the sun and I'm the moon
We can't collide
I would be obliterated by your heat
but at the same time
you are what completes me
In your absence
the days consist of endless gloom
however
you can be poison when there is too much of you
And although most days I can't get enough of your warmth
sometimes I prefer the shade
so I don't get burned

I don't exist on my own
but I must learn how to
So when I think about our love
you are the sun
and I'm the moon
We can't collide
but we chose to anyway
and now I am destroyed

The Breaking & the Blooming

Self-destruction portrays itself
in many forms
I guess one of mine was loving you
when you clearly
did not love me

The Breaking & the Blooming

I never believed in God
so tell me why
I am on my knees
praying for you to come back to me

The Breaking & the Blooming

Those hands crave me
but never seem to love me entirely
Those lips reek of desire
but lack consistency and fidelity
And I would be lying if I said I didn't settle
as long as I could feel you next to me
No matter the circumstance
I always felt at home
with the warmth of you
even if it was temporary
because at least our bodies
were existing under the same stars

The Breaking & the Blooming

My mistake was expecting that somehow
I could birth love
from lust
But I am a liability
searching for affection in places where it simply doesn't
belong
at the palms of those who simply can't reciprocate

I just want to be wanted
all the time
so I find myself caving into the arms of those
who have no intention of holding me
like they are afraid to lose me

The Breaking & the Blooming

Although your complexion is breathtaking
I refuse to compare it to the art that hangs among the pale
museum walls
You should not be rewarded with the luxury
of being depicted as a masterpiece

I cannot get lost in your eyes
the same way
I could get lost in *The Birth of Venus*
and I wouldn't stop and stare in awe
if I ever came upon them again
They're beautiful
but not that beautiful
The type of beautiful you notice for a moment
but forget days later because it serves no purpose

So I apologize for perceiving you as dull
I have learned to cherish more than appearance
once I got to know you
because beauty lies deeper than the structure of your jawbone
and your presence simply bores me

The Breaking & the Blooming

I have found that my worst griefs occurred right
in front of me

The lost connection between our souls
before they even knew
that they were lost

The Breaking & the Blooming

You are the reason I clutch onto those I love
just a little too tight now

*The uncertainty
has made a home inside me*

The Breaking & the Blooming

It hurts me to admit
that I would fall back into your arms
even after all this time
And sometimes
I hope that you don't come back
because I know I am not strong enough
to say no to you

The Breaking & the Blooming

I knew you had fallen out of love with me
when your arms no longer held me
like their biggest fear
was letting go

The hesitation of your hand in mine
like it had somewhere else
it would rather be
It was subtle
but I felt it in my bones

The Breaking & the Blooming

There was a war between our bodies
of whom could latch onto whom
tighter
you told me I would never win

Now here I am
fearing that I will never feel your grasp again
Winning that fight after all
but it rarely feels like a victory to me

The Breaking & the Blooming

There is nothing I find more beautiful
yet so tragic
than the cycle of the sun cascading beneath our feet
just so the moon can thrive
And the moon allowing the sun to take her place once again
so he can reflect his own light
But despite this
the two can never coexist
the aftermath
seemingly disastrous

I empathize
my only choice
is to love you from afar
because the moment I get too close
I'm afraid I will cease to exist

The Breaking & the Blooming

Whenever someone says
if they miss you
they'd call
I don't know whether to believe it
or not
Because every day since you left
your name tumbles in my mind
And I haven't sent a single text

The Breaking & the Blooming

I don't know how to look at you
without seeing poetry
But not the nice type
the type that will leave a bad taste on your tongue
long after it is digested
No matter how much shift
you will never settle comfortably in

My pen has never met soft words
and it won't start now
So if you think I am writing about you
I mean it in the most unflattering way possible

The Breaking & the Blooming

I give love
like the trees give oxygen
So if love doesn't exist like they say
where does that leave me

The Breaking & the Blooming

If there is indeed a life
after this one
will you search for me
until we meet again
and let our hearts intertwine
one last time

The Breaking & the Blooming

We didn't say one word to each other
the entire time that night
but your eyes

they told me
that they were forgetting me

The Breaking & the Blooming

Nothing in the world could have ever prepared me
for both the presence
and absence
of you

The Breaking & the Blooming

A part of me always knew we wouldn't make it
I felt it in your arms that one night
where your grip around me loosened
as you dozed off
Even your subconscious wanted to hold me tight
until it didn't
So I compromised
thinking back to every time you told me
you loved me
What was I wearing?
what was I doing?
what did my hair look like?
anything
to be that person again
And I've never been one to be angry
with change
But I thought that maybe this time
you'd never change your mind about me
until you did

The Breaking & the Blooming

I remember thinking
how could anything bad
come from feeling loved

The Healing

The Breaking & the Blooming

You called me difficult
like taking up space
was a bad thing
Like my only purpose
was to be small enough
to fit inside your back pocket
But I do not have the capacity to shrink
therefore
I will be felt for miles
and expand
as I please

The Breaking & the Blooming

I am both beauty
and destruction
I have been through hell
but you can't take your eyes
off me

You are the love
that made me forget
about anyone who had ever left

The Breaking & the Blooming

I wonder where I would be
if I had the desire to love me
the same way I had the desire
to love you

I would have anything
and everything

The Breaking & the Blooming

And if it were up to me
I would hold all your sadness
inside my hands
clutch it tightly
and make it my own
So that it never finds its way back to you
again

The Breaking & the Blooming

This poem
is an apology
for every single time
I picked apart my body in the mirror
like its entire existence
isn't to keep me alive
Like the fat on my stomach does not protect me
like the stretch marks on my thighs don't resemble my growth
like the hair on my legs does not keep me clean
It exists because I do
I exist because it does
Yet I continue to convince myself
it's against me
all the time

The Breaking & the Blooming

When we are skin on skin
it feels like our souls
are melting
into one

The Breaking & the Blooming

Stay away from people
who make you feel
like you need to shrink
Instead
let them choke

The Breaking & the Blooming

Your purpose on this earth
is not to serve as someone's void filler
And being lonely
will never suffice as an excuse
to forget who you are

I wish I could clone myself
somehow
I am the only one
who understands me

The Breaking & the Blooming

Love doesn't break you
a broken person does

The Breaking & the Blooming

I don't tell the universe
about just anyone
but I told her
about you
how your eyes are like the moon
and that I've wanted to be with the stars
ever since

The Breaking & the Blooming

The odds of existing
are slim
so the odds of you and I
existing at the same time
must be next to impossible
and I think that's beautiful
Maybe the universe does work in my favour
after all
because I got the chance to know you

The Breaking & the Blooming

Something I never quite understood
is why must we always be broken
before we can be loved
Why can we not be loved the right way
the first time around
Why do we have to fall into the arms of tragedy
after tragedy
before the universe realizes
we've had enough

The Breaking & the Blooming

I always found myself devoted to the moon
particularly because she reminds me of myself
She sits in utter silence
but her presence is never gone unnoticed
Whether the world is crumbling beneath her feet or not
she continues to prosper
She ignites even the darkest of skies
the same way my eyes ignite any crowded room
I step into

And I know the personal comparison to the moon might seem cliché
but when she falls so do I
when she's incomplete she's still breathtaking
and you always know she must rise again soon
And when she does
she makes damn sure her presence is felt

The Breaking & the Blooming

At first
I was scared that I was never going to find someone
like you again
but maybe that's not such a bad thing
after all
Because the moment I was more afraid of losing you
than losing me
was the moment I had already lost myself
But now I have the desire to love me
the same way I loved you
The only difference is you didn't deserve any of it
but I deserve it
all the time

The Breaking & the Blooming

I asked my heart today
if she remembers you
she does
but not in the way you might think
She remembers but she does not crave
when your name passes by
she doesn't cling to it like flies
She accepts your absence
but no longer prays for your return

The Breaking & the Blooming

If you lose me once
you won't ever lose me again
And I know that it is harsh to admit
that I was lying when I said I wished you well
but read between the lines
it's not that I am cold-hearted
it's just that you don't deserve it

The Breaking & the Blooming

I will allow flowers to bloom
in the parts of me
that I loathe the most
I am a garden
deserving of every sun ray
and tested with every rainfall
but even then
I come out stronger than before

The Breaking & the Blooming

I know it's cliché
but if colours were people
you would be yellow
A living personification of the sun
but still manage to put sunshine to shame

All your presence does is nourish
you make water look like poison
it just doesn't fuel the way you do

And I know it's cliché but if colours were people
you would be yellow
Not pink or purple or blue
yellow
because you always knew exactly how
to ignite the darkest parts of me

The Breaking & the Blooming

Those who are meant to remain
don't need our convincing

The Breaking & the Blooming

To the person who falls in love with me
I will not deny that many nights are spent crying
on the bedside
because the tone of your voice when you said goodnight
was unfamiliar from the night before
That sometimes I am quiet
not a single word
and the days that I am not
I ask a lot of questions
But if you happen to feel as if I am too much to handle
know that I am also too much to lose
and impossible to replace

The Breaking & the Blooming

I am not afraid of love
even after all this hurt
I can look heartache in its eyes
and say *try me*
But even then
I'll still have pools full of love to give
So don't come here expecting to ruin me
You won't show up in my dreams
and I definitely won't be falling apart on the bathroom floor
Because you can't break someone
who knows exactly what they have
to offer

The Breaking & the Blooming

I am told to love myself
but the moment I do
I am self-absorbed
just existing is an invitation for you
to tell me I'm pretty
but I can't agree with you
because if I do
I'm a whore
And the moment I crumble
I need therapy
emotionally unavailable with simply too much baggage
I can't be in two places at once
You want me to love me
but not too much
because cockiness is never cute
But you must be confused
It's not that cockiness is never cute
it's you thinking I only matter
if you say I do

The Breaking & the Blooming

You don't exist
just to please people

The Breaking & the Blooming

I mistook attention
for connection
Dancing across the thin line between missing you
and just missing somebody
I realized I missed the hands solely
and what they do
not the person those hands are attached to
because who will hold me when I am falling apart now

But I am tired of pursuing people
who aren't even half of me
just to escape my loneliness
Comfort doesn't exist in random palms
and I owe myself far more
than just a temporary touch

The Breaking & the Blooming

Not everyone who hurts you
is deserving of forgiveness
Even your hatred
is just a little too generous

The Breaking & the Blooming

I want to be closer than skin on skin
let me settle in between
the strands of your heart

The Breaking & the Blooming

I am absolutely and unapologetically falling in love
with the process of falling in love with me
something I used to perceive as unattainable
I convinced myself
that my entire being was determined
on whether you
loved me
But my heart does not beat for you
and even if it did
you would cave at the very sight of my intensity
and you did
I know now
that I am not hard to love
you just lack the strength it takes to love me
but I am flooding with it

The Breaking & the Blooming

I spent years hating my name
until I saw what it looked like
on your lips
how delicately it seeped out of the cracks
like honey
and tasted like it too

The Breaking & the Blooming

I found myself apologizing for how hard I love
to people who can't seem to stomach their own emotions
I apologized for the intensity of my love
to those whose lips couldn't even begin to formulate one of
their own
and God knows I have deserved one
Saying "you are too much for me"
as an insult
as if I didn't already know
I could sense your weakness by the way you kissed me
your hand didn't wrap firmly around my neck
and your eyes grew timid
when I wrapped mine around yours
You can't handle me
and I don't expect you to
So if you find yourself questioning
if you are for me
you probably are not

The Breaking & the Blooming

I never meant to neglect you
As if you were a hotel along an unknown road
comprised of temporaries
and nothing else to offer
besides a night stay
You are a home
with paintings plastered among the walls
that you could stare at for hours
and shelves full of books that you never fail
to get lost in
You are not cold and empty
you are kind and welcoming
and I'm sorry I didn't try to love you sooner

The Breaking & the Blooming

Maybe we must break
to rebuild
And maybe rock bottom
isn't rock bottom
after all
rather exactly what we need
to become whole again

The Breaking & the Blooming

I am not an inconvenience

The Breaking & the Blooming

I like to think
that even though we didn't work out
my love was not wasted
that you consumed as much warmth
as you could
before we fell to pieces
And I like to think
that no matter how we ended
you still feel it sometimes
I know I do

The Breaking & the Blooming

I am always worthy of being something
to somebody
even when I am nothing to myself

Especially then

Do you think about me
when your hands are around her neck
and wish it was me looking up at you
instead

The Breaking & the Blooming

When I looked into your eyes
for the first time
it made stargazing
seem dull

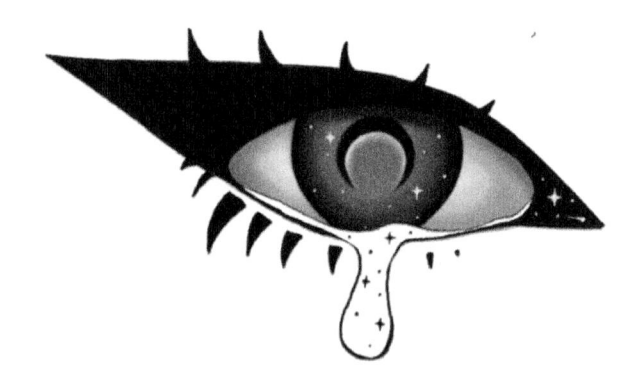

The Breaking & the Blooming

In that moment
I knew I had no choice
but to remain soft
No matter what
you did to me

Why do we eagerly place our hearts
in the hands of those
who can't comprehend our fragility

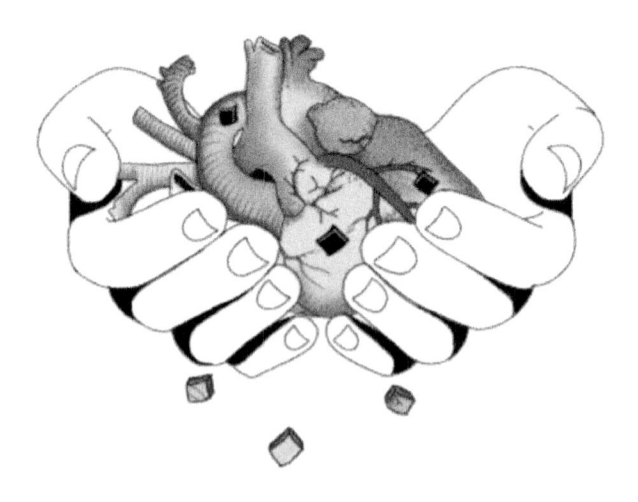

The Breaking & the Blooming

You make the world
feel a little less awful to me

The Breaking & the Blooming

Don't treat me like a river
in the woods
when I am the ocean sea
I consist of depth
and complexity
I am not a single quiet stream

The Breaking & the Blooming

You only loved me
with tear-stained cheeks
and trembling hands
Or when I was too anxious to get a word in
or when I stumbled at your feet
searching for healing
You only loved me
when I was coated in self-loathing
dripping in hatred
pouring out one tragedy
after another
because that meant putting you before me
viewing you
as the hero
And I refuse to do that
anymore

The Breaking & the Blooming

I can't tell if I have painted myself
as the villain
or the hero
I suppose I am both
I probably am both
because even though I have broken myself
a million times
I'm the only one who ever took the time
to mend the pieces

The Breaking & the Blooming

Will I ever get the soft love
that hugs you without arms
you can still feel their warmth when they're not near
The type of love where their kiss lingers on your skin
so much so you swear they're still there
Where you don't have to question
whether the love even exists
to begin with
they show you all the time
it's impossible to forget

I hope the world knows
that I can't handle the sad love anymore
I'm mad at myself for even calling it that
because love shouldn't make you want to rip your heart out
But here I am
holding it in my hands anyway
still willing to give it another shot
every single time

The Breaking & the Blooming

If I could hate so deeply
don't ever question the depth of my love
like it wouldn't drown you out in seconds

The Breaking & the Blooming

If you had left me years ago
I would have fallen apart
The world would crumble in my palms
I'd cave into the wreckage like silk
But now
I am the one who leads the way
there is no more hesitation in these bones

I guess it takes so much hurt
for the heart to realize
we don't need to break like this
anymore

The Breaking & the Blooming

Eventually you will come to find
that forcing them to be a part of you
will always feel so much lonelier
than just letting go

The Breaking & the Blooming

He didn't make me anxious
or sad
he made me feel safe
at home even
And that's the greatest love story
I will ever know

The Breaking & the Blooming

You did not break me
instead
you freed me

The Breaking & the Blooming

I do not wish you harm
however
I do wish you
everything that you deserve
and if that happens to be harm
so be it
but I won't sit here
and pray the worst for you
Because the worst for you is already true
you must live
with what you are
but you will never see me again

The Breaking & the Blooming

If I must love you
from afar
I will
and if I must love you
in utter silence
I will
Because although I can't seem to forget what we had
I want nothing
to do with you

The Breaking & the Blooming

I don't blame you anymore
for what you did
And I don't lay awake at night
picking apart who I was
and who I wasn't
I no longer try to rationalize why you hurt me
or question how you walked away so easily
because once I stopped making excuses
and searching for answers
it was no longer complicated
or a secret
or difficult to figure out
I know now that you don't have the capacity to love
You were never taught how
you never learned on your own either
And that has nothing
to do with me

The Breaking & the Blooming

I had the power to be anything
I wanted to be
and foolishly
all I wanted was to be loved
by you
to be held by you
to be touched by you
I could have wished for the moon
for the stars
but *no*
I wanted your mediocre love
that you made me feel undeserving of
But I guess
you were right
I am deserving of so much more
and I'm ashamed that I accepted
whatever you were willing
to give me

The Breaking & the Blooming

I am no longer accepting complicated love
You either love me softly
or not at all

The Breaking & the Blooming

Me without you
is simply
me
without
you
and that is all

The Breaking & the Blooming

Let go of anything
and everything
that disrupts
your gentleness

The Breaking & the Blooming

To deny love's existence
is to deny
my own

A thank you note

Whether you read this front to back all in one sitting, or you picked it up sporadically and read on your own timeline, thank you for always handling me with care. And thank you for allowing me to share these things with you, I wouldn't have wanted it any other way.

Printed in Great Britain
by Amazon